MONT-
SERRAT

Photos by Jaume Balanyà   Words by Maria Pilar Queralt
TRIANGLE POSTALS

Index

MONTSERRAT, THE SLEEPING DRAGON

From the air, Montserrat looks like a huge sleeping dragon. Steep scales of stone cover its flanks and the serrated outline of its backbone makes it impossible to distinguish its head from its tail. Perhaps its stone heart was wounded by the lance of the knight St. George – another distinguished emblem of the Catalan identity as he is Catalonia's patron saint – who first rescued the princess and then charged the dragon with guarding the two hidden treasures of the mountain, its monastery, with its cultural and religious heritage, and the natural environment that is unique because of its variety and beauty.

Situated 38 kilometres from Barcelona, close to the point where three districts – L'Anoia, El Bages and El Baix Llobregat – come together, the Montserrat sierra is full of the romantic and unusual charms that arise from legends thanks to its rare morphology, to the cultural and religious legacy that it provides shelter to, and to the frequent mists that blur outlines and mask any ruggedness. Its remarkable landscape that emerges and stands out from the rest of its surroundings has turned it into the source of legends, a tourist attraction, a spiritual nucleus and an important element in history. There are many ways of looking at the mountain. You will not be disappointed, whichever you choose.

HISTORY AND LEGENDS
GUARDIAN OF MEMORY

On 21 May 1858, when the newspaper *El Conceller* published *A la Verge de Montserrat* (To Our Lady of

Montserrat), the first poem in Catalan by the poet and politician Víctor Balaguer (1824-1901), the public adopted Montserrat as the symbol and emblem of the Catalan identity.

Symbolism apart, it is true that Montserrat combines its incomparable natural environment with its status as the living memory of the history of Catalonia, a history that begins in the Neolithic Period, when the first human settlements were established on the mountain. The mists of uncertainty surrounding those early signs of life clear with the testimony of remarkable pottery decorated with

Dusk on the
Coll del Migdia

impressions known as cardial or *Montserratina* pottery. The continuing presence of man on the mountain is shown by the Neolithic burials found at Collbató and the Iberian pottery discovered in the Cova Freda cave.

Montserrat emerges from this relative anonymity as a result of a legend which has it that in 880, some shepherds followed a constant bright light that appeared every Saturday at a particular point of the mountain. Accompanied by the bishop of Manresa, they went to the spot marked by the mysterious light and there, in a cave, now known as La Santa Cova (the Holy Cave), they found an image of the Virgin. A legendary tradition that would seem to be confirmed by documents dating from just eight years later that talk of the hermitages and shrines of Santa Maria, Sant Iscle, Sant Pere and Sant Martí being established on the mountain.

One of these, the hermitage of Santa Maria, could have been the seed of the coenoby founded in 1025 by Oliba, the abbot of Ripoll. The monastic nucleus grew rapidly and in the 12th century a Romanesque church was built. It was in this church that the carving revered today was enthroned. A century later, in 1233, the existence of the Brotherhood of Our Lady of Montserrat appears in documents, as does a boys' choir, the first children's choir to be formed in Europe.

Our Lady of Montserrat, popularly known as «La Moreneta» (the dark one)

The Santa Cova →

The monastery surroundings *c*. 1920
[Photos: Ramon Queralt Albi)

Two centuries passed before the monastery became an abbey in its own right, independent of Ripoll (1409), but this was short-lived as in 1499, Ferdinand the Catholic stipulated that the community should remain under the authority of the Congregation of San Benito el Real in Valladolid, a situation that continued until the 19th century. The abbot at the time of Ferdinand's decision was García de Cisneros, the writer of *Exercitatorio de Vita Spiritualis* and a man who promoted the monastic vocation through the culture inherent in the monastery. The best demonstration of this is the installation in 1490 of the monastery's own printing press.

At the same time, the mountain was home to a large number of hermits, the most famous of whom, Bernat Boïl, abandoned his life as a recluse to accompany Christopher Columbus on his second voyage to the Americas and who was responsible, as the first apostolic vicar in the Indies, for spreading the cult of Our Lady of Montserrat in the Americas. Not long afterwards, Ignatius of Loyola, the founder of the Society of Jesus, carried the name of Montserrat throughout the whole of Europe. So great was the devotion that in the 17th and 18th centuries foundations were set up under her avocation in Austria and Bohemia.

The political ups and downs of the 19th century, in particular the invasion of Napoleon's troops, brought war and desolation to Montserrat. It is said that when a shepherd in the municipality of El Bruc banged his drum, it resonated across the mountain and caused the French troops to flee as the echo made them believe that an army was approaching. Sadly, the truth of the fighting is sadder than legend would have it, as the war led to the destruction of the monastery and part of its impressive library. Mendizábal's law, implemented later and which led to the forced seizure of monastic property, did not augur well for the future of the monks.

As a result, when ownership of the monastery was restored to the monks in 1844, they found little more than a pile of rubble. It was Abbot Miquel Muntadas who began the reconstruction of the monastic complex in 1858 independently of the community in Valladolid. This work led to surroundings similar to those we see today. These, as we have seen, are the years when Montserrat and Our Lady of Montserrat began to incarnate the spirit of the most conservative Catalan identity. When the first millennium of the monastery's existence was celebrated in 1881, the Virgin, popularly known as "La Moreneta" (the dark one), was enthroned as the patron saint of Catalonia. To popularise the cult and to facilitate access to the monastery, the much loved cog train was built in 1892, and in 1915, at the initiative of Abbot Marcet, the First Liturgical Congress was held at Montserrat. Since then, the life of the mountain has gone hand in hand with the history of the country.

The Spanish Civil War signified spoliation and exile for the monks, just as it did for many Spaniards. When the conflict had come to an end, the leadership of Abbot Aureli M. Escarré brought about the restoration of the monastery, which became a bastion of Catalan culture at his instigation. In 1970, Montserrat played in active part in the resistance to Franco when it welcomed a gathering of more than 300 intellectuals calling on the dictatorship to respect human rights.

In recent decades, Montserrat has undergone a number of restoration projects that have made it suitable for welcoming a large number of pilgrims or visitors, one of them being John Paul II, who visited the monastery in 1982. At the present time, through the Fundació Abadia de Montserrat 2025, set up in 1997, Montserrat is getting ready to face the future and the challenges that the new times will bring.

← The monastery
surroundings c. 1920
[Photos: Ramon Queralt Albi]

Monument in memory →
of the El Bruc Drummer

And there's more to the mountain than history. Legends have also found a place amidst the steep summits of the sierra. In the past, there were those who believed that Montserrat was the repository of the mythical Holy Grail; more recently, some are convinced that it is a base for galactic travellers or an enclave for paranormal phenomena. Mystery seems to have taken possession of the sierra, yet the cause probably lies in the magnificent scenery formed by its lofty natural spires and the mists that create an ethereal and shifting curtain, hiding these spires from sight. It is true, nevertheless, that Montserrat is an important element in the popular memory.

One of these legends, and perhaps the best known as it has been turned into an opera, is that of the hermit Garí, whose renown as a saint reached the ears of no less than the Catalan count Wilfred the Hairy, who was looking desperately for a remedy for his daughter Riquilda, who he believed was possessed by the devil.

Father Garí.
Polychrome wooden
carving. 16th century.

The count went up to Montserrat but Garí had to seek the advice of a hermit who had newly arrived on the mountain before he would allow the young woman to be admitted into his cell as he was afraid that she would put an end to his life of chastity. Nor was he mistaken because the inevitable happened. In despair at his weakness and fearful of having to face the count's anger, he once again followed the advice of the neighbouring hermit and killed the girl. Barely had he buried her when Garí watched in horror as his companion hermit turned into the devil himself and then disappeared amidst a cloud of sulphur.

Time passed and nothing was heard of Riquilda or Garí until one day, some hunters dragged into court a strange beast that they had caught on Montserrat. When they presented it to Wilfred, a mysterious voice from the heavens spoke, saying, "Rise up, Garí, you are forgiven".

The creature was none other than the former hermit who, in order to expiate his sin, was living like an animal on all fours. He publicly repented and withdrew to Montserrat, where he lived an exemplary life of penitence and prayer.

Clearly, this is a mere legend, yet it must be said in its favour that it has a probable basis in fact, as it is claimed that some time in the 15th century, the monks took in a human creature living in a semi-wild state and gave him shelter and educated him.

In any event, the story is perpetuated in the Fra Garí vantage point, from which you can see a beautiful view of the monastery complex. This is an ideal spot to ponder on the charms of the legend and to feel the reverberations of the infinite whys and wherefores of history.

Dawn from Sant Jeroni →

THE MOUNTAIN
STONE GUARDIAN

Immutable in the face of adversity, the massif is affected by the action of just two sculptors, time and the weather, which have been patiently and ceaselessly carving out the mountain's unusual physiognomy.

The sierra seems to have originated from the sedimentation of materials deposited at the end of the Mesozoic Era by a fast-flowing river in a lake that filled central Catalonia. When part of the land subsided, the water flowed into the Mediterranean, the lake dried up and its bed was left exposed. From that time onwards, tectonic movements, erosion and meteorological phenomena have patiently worked the massif, giving it the form that we are familiar with today. This was not a difficult. The fragility of the calcareous material, allied with the hardness of the rocks, gave rise to the singular forms of the peaks we see today and to the creation of caves, chasms

View of Montserrat
from Marganell

and grottoes. The most important of these are undoubtedly the famous Salnitre caves, the entrance to which is at Collbató, a small town on the southern slope of the massif that was the birthplace of the renowned composer Amadeu Vives. The caves, which stretch for over half a kilometre and which are open to the public, contain numerous marvellous combinations of stalactites and stalagmites that adorn its various chambers. However, we should not forget other chasms on the mountain, some of which, such as La Costadreta (125 m) or Els Pouetons de les Agulles (140 m), are over 100 metres deep and are popular with lovers of potholing, a sport widely practised in the area.

The outcrops and ridges that make up the silhouette of the massif have seduced the towns and people who live around it, have fed their imaginations and have, with their curious names, given rise to a genuine literature of the landscape: Els Frares Encantats (the Enchanted Brothers), El Camell (the Camel), La Mòmia (the Mummy), El Cavall Bernat (the Horse Bernat), La Roca Foradada (the Pierced Rock), El Bastó del Frare (the Friar's Stick), El Novici (the Novice), L'Escorpí (the Scorpion) and others compete with the peaks named after the hermitages built on them by the hermits who lived there. Such is the case of Sant Joan, Sant Salvador (1,152 m) and Sant Jeroni, the very top of the sierra, at a height of 1,236 m above sea level.

The Salnitre caves, in the municipality of Collbató

This phantasmagorical character is Montserrat's chief attraction. Indeed its size would not make it a particularly noteworthy sierra – its surface area is around 45 km^2 and its peaks are less than 1,300 metres high – but its presence is impressive due to the sharp steepness of its sides and the lack in the immediate surroundings of any rival that might compete with it in height.

The municipalities of Collbató, El Bruc, Marganell and Monistrol de Montserrat are rivals in the administration of the massif. These small population centres are sheltered by the mountain and have experienced a dream lasting hundreds of years. Tourism has resulted in the expansion of all three through the construction of holiday camps and other properties where the residents of Barcelona seek refuge from the harsh heat of the summer and where they can forget, at least at the weekends, the hustle and bustle of the big city as they relax amidst incomparable natural surroundings.

Collbató   El Bruc Parish Church   Monistrol de Montserrat

← Plaça del Bo-Bo, in
Monistrol de Montserrat

A street in Collbató →

The irregular topography of the mountain creates the right conditions for tremendous changes in the weather. The result of this is the formation of numerous microclimates that have enabled an enormous variety of flora to flourish. Life is present on Montserrat in the form of plants that can withstand exposure to severe meteorological conditions, bushes that cling perilously onto rocks, and grasses that carpet the damp hollows and spread out under the sun on the peaks in an explosion of vigour and colour.

The serenely beautiful holm oaks rise up majestically amongst the rocks, and their green turns slightly grey from the reflection of the venerable stones. At their feet, the undergrowth pays homage to them, revealing the yellow flowers of the broom and perfumed by the sweet scent of rosemary and thyme, and dotted with delicate, tiny flowers.

So abundant and varied are the aromatic herbs here that the monks used to make a liqueur with them called *Aromas de Montserrat*. Yew trees, oaks and pines add to the splendid palette of greens made up of the hues of more than 1,250 different species.

Els Gorros and
Magdalenes, in the area
of Santa Magdalena

Running freely amongst the trees are weasels, foxes, wild boar, badgers and Pyrenean goats which proudly stand atop the steepest of rocks, heedless of the danger. All the while, the sky is filled with wood pigeons, blackbirds and crows; the owl, the mythical emblem of Pallas Athene, is a sign of the wisdom concealed by the mountain, while the solitary eagle flies above the peaks.

Ever since the first inhabitants settled on the mountain in prehistoric times, its dangers have proved a hypnotic allure for man. A popular spot with mountain climbers, ever since the early days of the rambling and mountaineering movement, it has offered up its natural beauties to all those looking for rest, sport, adventure or the pleasures of the landscape. Rarely does one come across a climber who has never tried to reach the top of one of its peaks. The first ropes were organised around 1922 and in 1935 Cavall Bernat was conquered. The following year, the top of El Cilindre (the Cylinder) was reached and in 1948 the peak of Sant Jeroni felt man's foot for the first time. In 1955, those who sought to scale La Paret dels Diables (the Devils' Wall) were rewarded by triumph and even now getting to the top of one of its peaks is highly regarded amongst climbing circles, even though the Generalitat de Catalunya (the Government of Catalonia) declared the mountain a natural park on 29 January 1987, since when the appropriate measures have been put in place to ensure that the environment is undamaged by the sport.

Forest rangers in the area
of Les Agulles

Climbers roped together
on La Mòmia

Nevertheless, Montserrat must be experienced, with, of course, the due precautions. If you want to discover the secret charms of the mountain, you need to put on a good pair of walking boots and get lost while wandering along its paths, lean over the dizzying drops of its sheer sides and fall in love with the seasonally changing hues of the landscape.

One reason for an outing might be to enjoy the magnificent panoramic views to be had from Montserrat of the plain of El Bages and the lower reaches of the Llobregat River. Another motive might be to find the countless hermitages and shrines dotted about the mountain. And the ideal way to achieve both of these is to climb up to the top of Sant Joan (976 m) by means of the convenient funicular that starts off from the monastery. Once at the top, at the so-called Plaça de les Taràntules, take the path that leads to the Chapel of Sant Joan. Return to the path, which is a narrow track winding amidst rocks and holm oaks and which leads to the chapel and two small constructions that are built in such a way as to take advantage of a hollow in the rock. These are the hermitages of Sant Joan and Sant Onofre. A little further off is the shrine of Santa Caterina, which is also built into the rock and is half hidden by the vegetation. Undaunted, set out a little further up to the vantage point of Sant Joan at 1,957 m above sea level. From there you can see the fantastical forms of the Les Agulles massif, the stone organ that sends forth its notes over El Penedès and from where, on a clear day, you can see as far as El Montsant.

Shrine of Sant Salvador

Shrine of Sant Benet,
below L'Elefant

Another possibility to rebuild your body and your spirit is to start out from Sant Joan and conquer the peak of Sant Jeroni. This path is highly recommended. With the woodland as a natural barrier between the path and the abyss, walkers should allow themselves to be swallowed up by the huge stone crests and play at espying a series of tiny hermitages and shrines – Sant Dimes, Sant Benet, La Santa Creu, La Santíssima Trinitat and Sant Salvador – some of which appear in documents dating from the 12th century.

Even if you are on your own, you will not be lonely as the song of the air will whistle as you pass through the rocks to keep you company, and El Cavall Bernat will keep a watchful eye over you as you make your way between holm oak groves till you stand atop the highest peak of the massif. Before you get there, at 1,130 m above sea level, you will come across the Chapel of Sant Jeroni, which was built in 1891 on top of the ruins of an earlier chapel destroyed by Napoleon's troops in 1811. The reward for all your efforts will come at 1,236 m above sea level, when the vantage point at the top gives you a panoramic view that stretches from the Pyrenees to the Mediterranean. It is said that on clear days you can even make out the island of Mallorca.

While the panoramic view may be captivating, the 600 m sheer drop from the look-out point is dizzying. At the bottom, as if it were holding up the mountain, is the mass of trees surrounding El Bruc, the hamlets of Monistrol and Can Massana, the Romanesque Chapel of Santa Cecília and a string of needles, historic or natural pillars of the sierra that from this height seem altogether less haughty. There are a thousand and one paths that criss-cross the mountain, tracks that have been explored since time immemorial but which still retain the thrill of an adventure and the unique harmony of nature for those who wander along them.

Area of Les Agulles

← The Church of Sant Esteve, Marganell

Can Tobella farmhouse →

Can Jorba farmhouse → →

‹ View from Els Ecos

↑ Shrine of Sant Pau Vell   Area of Les Agulles ›

Various views of the
area of Les Agulles

View of Montserrat →
from the Coll del Bruc

La Cadireta d'Agulles

La Cadireta d'Agulles →
and La Roca Foradada

← The area of Les Agulles seen from Els Frares Encantats

↑ Coll de Les Agulles

Northern slope of the area
of Les Agulles

←← The face wall of
Les Agulles seen from
Collet de Guirló

← View of the Serrat
de la Portella

↑ Els Gorros seen from
El Bruc

La Bola de la Partió
and La Bitlla, in the area
of Les Agulles

Footpath from
Can Massana to Collet
de Guirló

Collet de Guirló, in ⁊
the area of Les Agulles

← La Monja and El Lloro,
in the area of Els Frares
Encantats

↑ Serrat del Moro,
seen from the Monastery
of Santa Cecília

Montserrat, →
the north slope

←← Coll del Migdia and the Sant Jeroni vantage point

← Coll del Migdia and the Talaia needle

↑ View of Montgròs from the Sant Jeroni vantage point

El Gegant Encantat seen → from the Sant Jeroni vantage point

69

←← Serrat del Patriarca and the Sant Jeroni face wall   ← The Sant Jeroni face wall   ↑ The area of Sant Benet   Els Flautats →

← La Prenyada and La Mòmia

La Boleta del Portell Estret →
seen from the Coll de les Agulles

Els Pallers →
La Nina and La Boleta Foradada
El Cap de Mort
El Bisbe

Els Frares Encantats seen from Marganell →→

← Els Gorros covered in snow

↑ Bauma dels Plecs del Llibre

Els Plecs del Llibre →

El Cavall Bernat, the face
wall of Els Diables and the
Serrat del Patriarca

El Cavall Bernat →

Various views
of El Cavall Bernat

← The Monastery of Sant Benet seen from El Cavall Bernat

← Bauma de l'Arcada

El Serrat del Moro →

View of the area of →
Les Agulles at night

MONASTERY AND BASILICA
THE SOUL OF THE DRAGON

If the mountain is the vigilant dragon watching over memories of old and the physical environment, the

soul of the sleeping beast is, unquestionably, the monastery and the basilica. When the traveller reaches the great esplanade that leads up to the monastery, the first sensation is one of confusion.

The architectural eclecticism that welcomes the new arrival distracts the gaze and it is impossible to know whether you should fix on the St. George by Josep M. Subirachs (1986), the stepped squares designed by Josep Puig i Cadafalch in 1929, the remains of the old Gothic cloister, or the monastery's new façade built by Francesc Folguera between 1942 and 1968. The feeling of surprise

Montserrat Monastery

continues as you cross the threshold into the basilica and discover a Gothic portal and two sepulchres in the vestibule, which, together with the great Romanesque entrance of the old church, call to mind the ancient past of the monastery complex. And there is more to come. In the atrium of the basilica is a series of sgraffiti produced in the 1950s and an image of St. Ignatius of Loyola by the sculptor Rafel Solanic (1895-1990), which coexist in the same space with a 17th-century stone tablet commemorating the saint's vigil on Montserrat on 25 March 1552 and a number of pieces of contemporary sculpture, three of which – of John I of Aragon, Charles I and St. Gregory the Great – are the work of Frederic Marès (1883-1991).

Montserrat therefore lacks the Romanesque austerity or Gothic elegance of the great monasteries of medieval times, yet there is something indefinable in the atmosphere, a special magnetism that surpasses any possible aesthetic shortcomings and which attracts the visitor into the basilica. It is enough to go through the magnificent Neo-Baroque façade designed by the Venanci brothers (1828-1919) and Agapit Vallmitjana (1830-1905) to understand the mystery.

A single nave, as a result of the transition from the Gothic to the Renaissance and restored in the late 19th century, presents to the traveller its ostentatious Neo-Byzantine decoration with touches of *Modernisme* and symbolism that make up a complex, elaborate and eclectic whole. It is, therefore, a space far removed from current aesthetic sensibilities, but you are, nevertheless, moved by something indefinable, which must unquestionably be the energy of a people, the good intentions of so many simple folk who have come to the basilica in search of peace and tranquillity. A collective catharsis of the spirit that distracts the attention from the walls and columns and leads the gaze up to the sober 12th-century carving on its silver throne, presiding over the nave. If at the same time

Plaça de Santa Maria,
designed by
Josep Puig i Cadafalch

you can hear the sweet voices of the Escolania choir, then so much the better. The voices of these 50 or so boys act as a purifying filter, stripping bare the walls, leading us to ignore any artifice and resulting in an internalisation of emotions and sentiments.

The basilica is modest in size as the central aisle measures just 58 metres long, 15 wide and 23 high. The effect of width comes from the numerous side chapels, one of which, that of the Holy Sacrament, has recently been restored (1977) by Subirachs. In the presbytery, decorated with *Modernista* paintings by Alexandre de Riquer (1856-1920), Joaquim Vancells (1856-1942) and Joan Llimona (1860-1926), are various scenes depicting the legend of Montserrat, together with scenes from the life of the Virgin.

To reach the niche room of Our Lady, you go directly from the atrium through a solemn alabaster door sculpted by Enric Monjo and unveiled in 1954. The room where the image of the Virgin is revered is completely covered with Venetian mosaics that surround the silver frontal made in 1947 in the style of an altarpiece by the goldsmiths Ramon Sunyer (1889-1963) and Alfons Serrahima (1906-1988). Alongside the room is the niche room proper, which is a chapel consisting of three Neo-Romanesque apses constructed between 1876 and 1885 and on which a very young Gaudí

The Neo-Baroque façade
of the basilica

Inside the basilica

(1852-1926) collaborated when he was just a simple assistant helping Francesc de Paula del Villar (1828-1921), the architect responsible for the works. The paintings on the dome, by Joan Llimona, are particularly worthy of note.

To return outside, you must take the so-called "Path of the Hail Mary", a passageway between the basilica's exterior façade and the rock of the mountain covered by a roof of methacrylate designed in 1982 by the architect Josep M. Martorell. This path could easily be described as luminous because the numerous candles offered by the pilgrims who come to see the Virgin create small explosions of light on the surface of the stone and produce an oneiric, enveloping atmosphere.

Montserrat's spirituality has not come about solely because it is a religious enclave, as the spirit is also nurtured by culture and the arts, and there is a considerable amount of both of these in the sierra.

Ever since it was founded, the monastery has been an important cultural focal point. The community of monks follows the Benedictine Rule, written by Benedict of Nursia in the 6th century, and even though their daily routine is marked by the liturgy, they also have an obligation to welcome pilgrims and to promote intellectual labours. Thus, while some monks are charged with undertak-

The niche room of
the image of Our Lady
of Montserrat

Detail of the image of
Our Lady of Montserrat.
Late 12th century

ing domestic or pastoral duties, others devote themselves to research in the fields of history, theology, philosophy and biblical studies. A prime example of this is the monastery and the museum's excellent publication's service. This arose from the love of one monk, Bonaventura Ubach (1879-1960), for architecture. During a number of visits to the Middle East, when he was involved in archaeological projects and worked on biblical studies, he gathered together a large number of pieces from the cultures of Mesopotamia, Egypt, Cyprus and the Holy Land. This collection grew through the addition of an excellent selection of Catalan painting and sculpture from the 19th and 20th century, including works by Rusiñol, Casas and Nonell, which are to be found alongside pieces by artists such as Miró, Picasso and Dalí. The French Impressionists are represented by Monet, Degas, Sisley and Pissarro, and there are American artists, such as Singer Sargent, and a number of Spanish painters, including Sorolla, Zuloaga and Romero de Torres. The pictorial past of Europe is represented by a collection acquired in Italy shortly after the end of the First World War that includes works by Caravaggio, Luca Giordano and Tiepolo.

Bonaventura Ubach was also responsible for the initiative to set up Montserrat's Scriptorium Biblicum, which translated the Bible into Catalan from the original sources. This alone more than demonstrates the cultural work undertaken at Montserrat, but mention must also be made of the importance of the monastery's philological and theological studies, the quality of its publications and the fidelity of its musical recordings, which have made the monastery one of the most important centres of Catalan culture.

The monastery is, of course, a private complex to which access is restricted. Puig i Cadafalch was involved in its reconstruction in 1925 and sought to give the premises the atmosphere and sense of

Inside one of the rooms
in the museum

The monastery gardens

The reading room
in the library

seclusion typical of Romanesque buildings, although to achieve this he used an original combination of stone, brick and wood.

Only the library is open to scholars and researchers by prior request. Considered one of the finest libraries in Europe, it contains more than 250,000 volumes, including some 400 incunabula and over 2,000 manuscripts, one of which is the famous *Llibre Vermell* (Red Book), an illuminated codex dating from the 14th century.

The monastery gardens are an oasis of peace away from the comings and goings of the tourists and pilgrims who invade the area. Pergolas, small lakes and tree-lined paths that head out towards the crags augur an atmosphere of absolute peace and silence.

Though visitors may not enter the gardens, they can instead find similar serenity by following the Way of the Cross. This starts out from Plaça del Abat Oliba and has monuments along the way, marking each of the episodes of the Passion. The current path replaces the original design by Enric Sagnier and Eduard Mercader, realised between 1904 and 1919 and which was, apart from the Chapel of La Soledad and the Chapel of La Dolorosa, destroyed during the Civil War.

Another pleasant itinerary within the monastery complex itself is the path of Els Degotalls (the Trickles), which begins at the monument erected in 1931 in homage to Jacint Verdaguer, who wrote the words for the *Virolai*. The path wanders amidst fountains, sculptures and majolica slabs before coming to a hollow in the rock from which the path takes its name. This cavity is a curious formation through which water from the mountain trickles on damp days.

Lastly, the visitor should head for La Santa Cova because it is here that tradition has it that the image of Our Lady of Montserrat was found. The walk is a pleasant stroll along which you can enjoy art and the beautiful panoramic views that will catch you unawares as you tread the path of history. The route is a wide path cut through the rock that was begun as far back as 1693 and concluded in 1704, but which was plagued with difficulties during its construction due to the steepness of the terrain and the limited technological advances of the period.

In the early years of the 20th century, the route was embellished with a Monumental Rosary with pieces produced by artists such as Puig i Cadafalch, Llimona, the Vallmitjana brothers and Gaudí himself. Between them they created the most important open-air work of *Modernista* sculpture in Barcelona.

At the end of the path is the construction that indicates the place where, according to legend, the image of Our Lady of Montserrat was found. In a perfect symbiotic relationship between architecture and nature, this site is in evident contrast with the sumptuousness of the monastery but exceeds it in beauty and spirituality.

Following the same purpose of going back to the origins of the monastery and the mystery of Montserrat, you should continue on to the Shrine of Santa Cecília, one of the most beautiful buildings in the early Catalan Romanesque style. Built in the 10th century, it has three apses decorated with Lombard arches and is used by the monks as a centre to welcome pilgrims.

You will now be able to consider your visit as complete. In your memory you will hold the vision of a unique landscape; in your soul will be a comforting feeling of peace. The dragon, meanwhile, will continue his secular snooze, keeping the promise he made to St. George that he would ensure the continuing survival of the heritage he was charged with protecting.

Monument to Jacint
Verdaguer on the
Els Degotalls footpath

← View of the monastery from El Cairat

← Aerial view of Montserrat Monastery

← The Sant Joan funicular

View of the monastery → from La Santa Cova footpath

The first station on the → Way of the Cross with monuments along the path, designed by Francesc Folguera

«The Resurrection». →→ Mystery of Glory along the path of the Monumental Rosary

Inside the cloister →
of La Santa Cova

View of La Santa Cova →→

Vantage point →
overlooking the Llobregat
River, with a sculpture by
Josep M. Subirachs

← Detail of the Neo-Baroque façade designed by Venanci and Agapit Vallmitjana

← View of part of the atrium of the Basilica of the Virgen de Montserrat

The basilica's atrium → and Neo-Baroque façade

Inside the basilica

The Montserrat choir

Devotion to
«La Moreneta» knows
no borders

Baptismal font

Monks from the
community during Mass

← Arcades in the Gothic cloister →

The cloister inside →
the monastery designed
by Puig i Cadafalch (1925)

← Father Oriol Diví,
working on the box trees

← Father Adalbert
Franquesa

↑ The library

The Montserrat choir →

← The monastery gardens

↑ Shrine of Sant Iscle, in the monastery gardens

← Shrine of La Santíssima
Trinitat, in the Monastery
of Santa Cecília

← Below. The shrines of
Sant Jeroni and Sant Benet

↑ The Church of Sant
Esteve, Marganell

Jaume Casals,
from the Guixà foundry,
Monistrol de Montserrat

Albert Blancafort,
an organ-maker
in Collbató

A view of the monastery
at dusk from the Fra Garí
vantage point

TRADUCTION
Susan Brownbridge

GRAPHIC DESIGN
Joan Colomer

EDITING
Serveis Editorials Estudi Balmes, SL

PHOTOMECHANICS
JAMSA

PRINTING
Grup 3, s.l.

LEGAL REGISTRATION
B-32141-2002

ISBN
84-8478-068-6